This is _____'s

Money Magnet
Coloring Book
& Prompt Journal

Started on _____

Completed _____

Get your financially abundant life off to a great start, or send it lovingly off on the next phase of your prosperous journey with these meditative coloring pages, and affirmation prompt pages.

The coloring pages are blank on the back so that you can remove them and use the images as art and inspiration somewhere you can see regularly.

In the journaling section, write whatever comes to mind when you read the affirmations for abundance and prosperity.

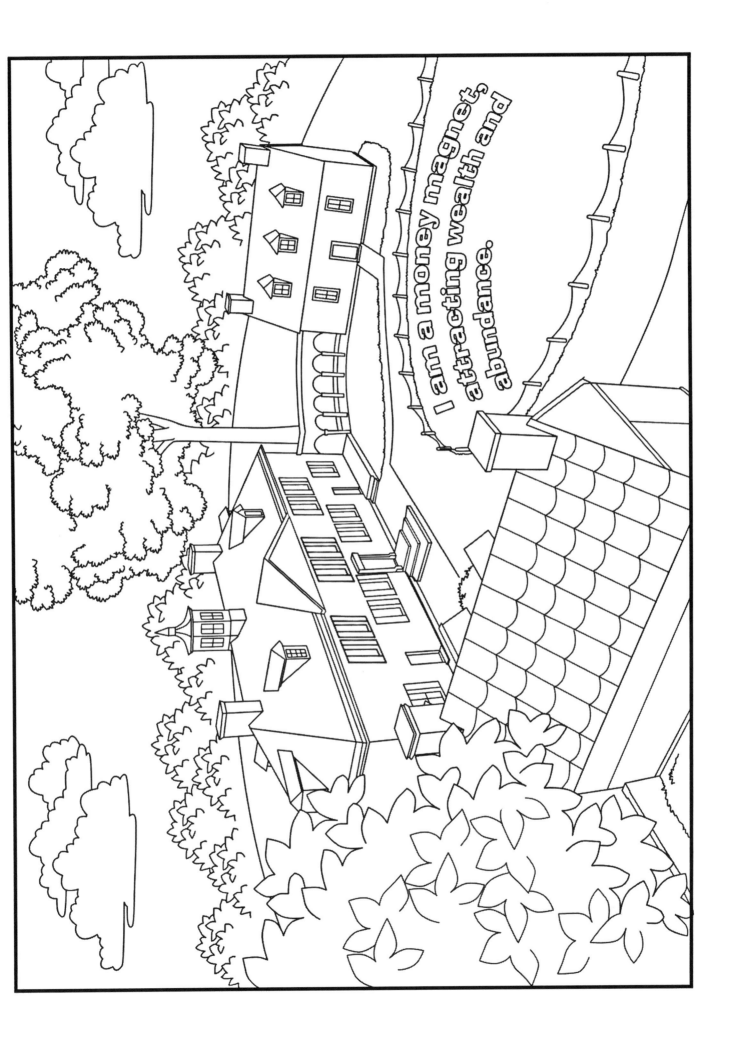

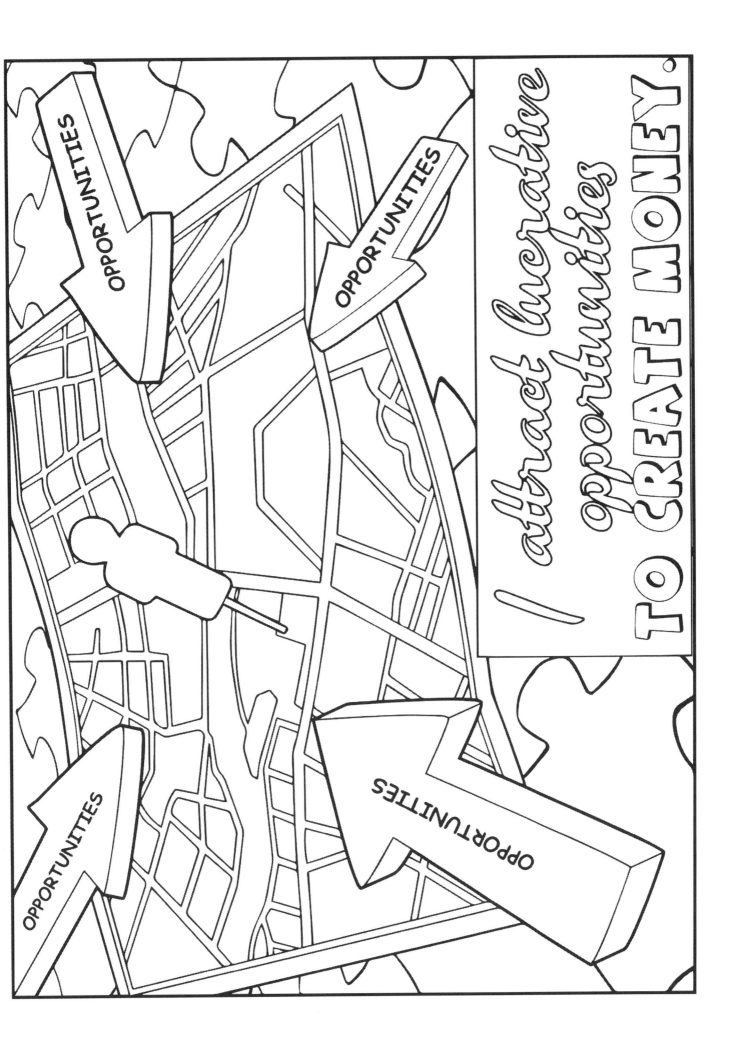

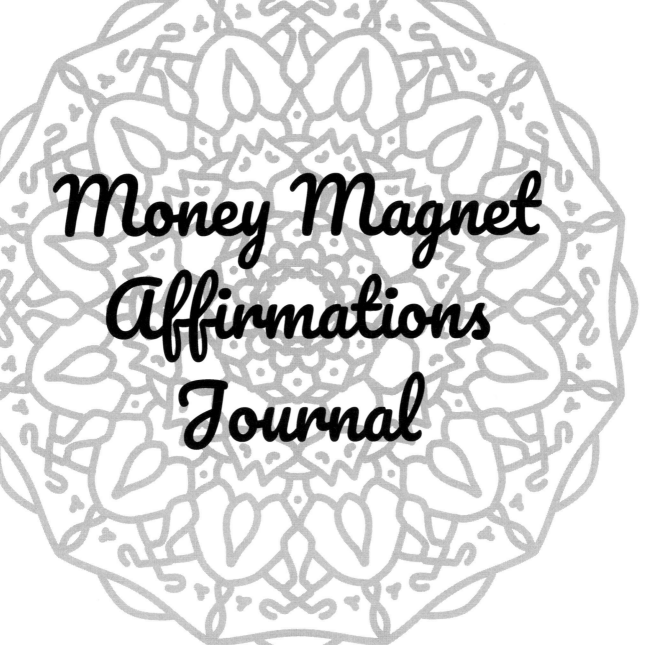

I attract money effortlessly and easily

I continuously discover new avenues of income

I am grateful for this moment which enriches my life

I am more and more prosperous every day

I use money to better other people's lives

My life is full of prosperity

I always receive exactly what I ask for and am appreciative of it

I deserve abundance and prosperity

I am open to all the wealth life has to offer

I manage my money wisely

I am destined to find prosperity in everything I do

I am grateful for my abundant prosperity

I maintain my wealth so I can help others

My abundance is generated within me

I am a money magnet, attracting wealth and abundance

I pay bills before they are due to share the wealth with the company's employees

I experience gratitude for everything I have in my life

I deserve the very best life has to offer

I am responsible for being a good steward of the abundance and wealth provided

I am surrounded by abundance

I am thankful for the abundance I have in my life

I attract lucrative opportunities to create money

My daily attitude is one of gratitude

Abundance flows to me freely and easily

I am a magnet for all good and I am grateful for it

I see abundance everywhere

My gratitude and appreciation attracts abundance of every kind

I rejoice for others who are prosperous and share the abundance

Made in the USA
Columbia, SC
20 November 2020